Connected Conversations

Tiffany Street

Copyright Notice © 2023 Tiffany Street,

All rights reserved, including any right to reproduce this book or portion thereof in any form whatsoever.

This book is designed to provide accurate and authoritative information concerning the subject matter covered. It is sold with the understanding that the content is expressly written from experiences throughout the author's life.

For information on bulk orders, contact Tiffany Street at briana8987@yahoo.com.

ISBN: 979-8-9878587-0-7

Disclaimer

This book is designed to bring awareness to various matters in life. The author does not claim that the experiences shared within the book are ones that the reader will experience or have experienced. The information shared within this book highlights a few difficulties and drawbacks that the author experienced and how she overcame them. Sound efforts have been made for content accuracy. You hereby agree never to sue or hold the author liable for any claims or similarities arising from the information contained within this book. Any likenesses to real persons, alive or deceased, or personal experiences are merely coincidental. You agree to be bound by this disclaimer.

Dedication

Thank you to the many people that have touched my life, shaped my thought process, and enlightened my spirit. I dedicate these words to you. It was only fitting as your conversations inspired them.

I have always had a love-hate relationship with the human race. For the most part, I love people. However, certain persons throughout my life have made me question my willingness to be open to the conversations that strangers provide. Since being touched by many people during my almost 34 years, I realize we learn from the ones that hurt us. Honestly, we learn the most from the ones who hurt us. After all, they taught us how to love. Perhaps not at the stage we wanted, but that's all a part of growth.

So, thank you to anyone who came into my life. No matter if your purpose was to shake it up temporarily, which typically would produce long-term mindset expansion, or if you hurt me. In most ways, the hurt helped me become

Connected Conversations

someone of permanence in this world of fleeting happiness and temporary highs and lows.

To my people, I appreciate you for every emotion your presence prompted and every decision your conversation inspired.

WHAT'S INSIDE

Disclaimer iii
Dedication iv
Notes Of Love ix
Foreword xvii
Introduction 1

LOSS 4
Trauma Groomed 5
Second Chances 8
Fooled 11
Daddy Issues 13
Just Pull Back 16
You're Gonna Want Me Back 17
I Woke Up Today 19
Dear Love 21
Take Note 23
The Awareness Moment ~ Journal Entry 24

LOVE 26
Twin Flame 27
Five Steps To Loving Me 29
Lucky One 31
In The Moment ~ Journal Entry 33
Choices 35
Luminescent Light 38
In The Moment ~ Journal Entry 40
In The Moment ~ Journal Entry 42

OBSTACLES 44
Hi Mom 45
Breathe 47
Roller Coaster 52
The Boundaries Moment ~ Journal Entry 53
Non-Responsive 56
Goodbye 58
The Boundaries Moment ~ Journal Entry 60

VICTORY 63
Rescue Rope 64
Always Turn The Page 66
The Decisive Moment ~ Journal Entry 71
Vulnerability 74
The Decisive Moment ~ Journal Entry 76
The Decisive Moment ~ Journal Entry 81
About the Author 84

Notes Of Love

Tiffany has always been someone I held dear to my heart. From the first time I met her, I immediately noticed her genuineness and how she could light up the room. People (including myself) gravitated toward her. She was not afraid to tell you like it was, but she also seemed to care about everyone. Her heart is so big that she would take on other people's problems as people would often open up to her. She has a unique gift of loving others when most people don't care. This book is a prime example of her love for others by sharing her heart and vulnerability to reach people at their core. I am so proud of you Calle, and I love you so much.

Sam

Connected Conversations

2004(ish). French class.

You had your head in a textbook for an entire semester before we spoke. It was not because the book was so fascinating, but because it was easier to stay hidden in plain sight than make new friends - at yet another new school.

Yet, we were assigned as project partners; the rest is history—an instant bond. A bond built upon teenage inquisitiveness, a love for books and reading, unspoken family hardships, and hope for the future we would write for ourselves.

A friendship for the ages.

Love. Breakups. Promotions. Deaths. Births.

We've been through it all.

Question: What is more important, the journey or the destination?

Answer: The company.

I have loved being on this ride of life with you thus far, and I am excited to see where it leads us. We always talked about writing books one day. I am proud of you for pursuing your goals even when they may have seemed unattainable. Continue to shine your light on this world that sometimes gets too dark. Love you!

XoXo

Atousa

Notes Of Love

To my dear sister,

I have loved watching you pursue your dreams and am so proud of you for seeing them to fruition with this book's release. You always strive for excellence and have passion for your work. Your strength and determination continue to inspire those around you.

Thank you for being a person whom my daughter can look up to. You are such a beacon in the life of others and have helped many in their careers throughout your life journey.

Continue reaching for the stars, my love. There are many more great things to come for your future, and I look forward to being right there with you and seeing your dreams come true!

Love always, your big sister,

Amber

Connected Conversations

My love note to you,

I have a terrible memory. So, I don't remember the exact moment or day I met Tiffany, although I wish I did. What I do remember, however, is how I felt being in her presence. That feeling I will never forget.

I immediately felt safe, and the contagious, charismatic energy that she gives is absolutely beautiful. I was drawn to it. We instantly became friends, and she was the friend I wanted to tell my problems to, although I had other friends I had known longer. Why? Because Tiffany has a way of feeling like a safe place to both strangers and friends.

I have had the privilege of listening to some of her poems, and as I told Tiffany, her words feel like home. Her words have a way of feeling so profound. Her words pull you in so that your imagination can draw a picture of what she is describing.

I am incredibly proud of you, Tiffany! I will forever cherish you, and am honored to be your friend. You mean more to me than my average words could ever say. Thank you for sharing your vulnerability and heart of gold with the world.

Vivian

Notes Of Love

Tiffany,

As you turn 34, keep reaching until you take hold of what you seek. Feel it. Allow it. Breathe these feelings deeply and smoothly as you reach with a sure and fluid movement. Yield to the pain. Yield to what appears to be a distraction and move smoothly through as a snake sheds its skin.

Know that every encounter in every moment, including and most importantly, the ones you spend with yourself, are exactly as you created them to be. You create magic. You are magic. Just be, and like a tree, you will naturally reach towards the light and the sun. JUST reach, no forcing, BUT stretching and allowing. Reaching through AND knowing while enjoying the journey. Know that your capabilities are endless. You are not only a spark of God. You are a GODDESS.

Your Mother,

Tanya

Connected Conversations

Tiffany,

For as long as I can remember, my favorite quote has been…

"Life is short, and we do not have much time to gladden the hearts of those who journey the way with us, so be swift to love and make haste to be kind." But never have I known a person that embodies this more than you, Tiffany. What started as a random act of kindness on your behalf is now one of my most cherished relationships. I am privileged to be on this journey of life and friendship with you.

Jenny

Notes Of Love

Dear Tiffany,

You deserve the world, and you have not always seen that.

I am honored to have been afforded the opportunity of a front-row seat for the past six years of your life. Thank you for deciding we were going to be best friends; my life would be drastically different without the presence of a sunflower constantly blooming.

I am beyond proud to say that you are starting to see that you do, in fact, deserve the world, and it is right at your fingertips.

Your growth as a person, friend, daughter, sister, coworker, community leader, writer, and aunt (to name a few), has been astounding. If I could, I would give you the ability to see yourself through all our lenses so that you could realize how truly special you are to those your presence touches in this world.

Keep reaching for the stars, leading with love, and don't forget to give yourself some grace. Enjoy this journey, and know that you are EXACTLY where you need to be.

Love,

Hannah Buckman

Connected Conversations

For a woman as strikingly gorgeous as you, it says a lot that the most beautiful parts of you lie beneath the skin's surface.

I am in constant awe of your strength to navigate life's peaks, valleys, and intricacies with such grace.

I take great pride in calling you a friend and now my extended family.

Delicate is defined as "…of intricate workmanship or quality." Please, continue to be the delicate wordsmith you so confidently are.

I love you wholly and completely.

Love,

Mo

Foreword

Expression is an art that births connection. It helps humanity find its way through the stories of others, whether it's dance, fashion, writing, attitude, drama, or even conversations. We find ourselves in the chosen artistic expression of others.

In this book, you'll find a masterful expression of deep thoughts, complex emotions, and heartfelt tales for every person to relate. Tiffany's greatest strengths in her creative work lie in how she expresses her inner world and how often her inner and outer worlds bleed together for one incredible emotional journey.

Her poetic style will capture your attention and tug thoughtfully on your heartstrings, reminding you of your greatest heartbreaks but also your greatest triumphs. But, most of all, what you'll gain from this collection of writing is the permission to be honest about how it feels to express your truth, to love like there is no tomorrow, and to freely connect with others over what it means to be you.

Connected Conversations

This is something Tiffany has always done so well. Her storytelling is reflective of her true emotions and unique experience. Her expression throughout the pages of *Connected Conversations* will inspire you to do the same.

Erika Giles
Digital Content Manager

Introduction

Men and women complain about the same things when it comes to dating. We both want space and attention. Do you see how these words contradict? How can we expect consistency without attention? Then, in the same breath, expect space before even having a respective level of attention. We are stubborn in ensuring we don't look like a "simp," as my niece would say. Therefore, both parties try to play it cool, never letting the other fully know their interest, never showing all their cards, thus never getting to play their hand. Then the hamster wheel begins. We date the one who is NOT, I repeat NOT, playing it cool, and of course, we love to hate him because it is not coming from the "right person," and by right, I mean the toxic one hiding cards and bread-crumbing us.

I have realized and believe I need a happy medium of space and attention. It's a science. The timeframes of when I need more attention could vary based on life circumstances.

Connected Conversations

You know what? Men are right. Women are complicated, but I am sure that is a human thing regardless of sex. I decided the one giving me too much attention, ain't it, even though he could have been. Hello, trauma responses. Alas, we meet again.

Let me explain my mental status at this present moment. I want to connect, relate, and vibe with you. With so many resources that create safe spaces and support groups, we can never have too many. Safe spaces are connections based on time, space, and circumstance of the day. You can have many connections. They are not differentiated by people but by the moments you spend with them. Our time with people creates opportunities to connect, relate, and relinquish pretenses. Each of these times is ever-changing and, therefore, deserving of its (own) separate connection.

My purpose is for individuality. I desire that you listen, read, relate, laugh, cry, cringe, and connect with me individually based solely on your perception of my words. I took half a day from work, came to historic Fort De Soto Beach, and got inspired by the quiet. Of course, it was

Introduction

not completely quiet on a Tuesday's hot summer day in Florida. A frustrated mother was chasing after her adorable 2-year-old, but that didn't matter. It was quiet enough for me. For the first time in nine months, I could breathe. I laid back, allowing the waves to carry me out. My eyes were closed, and my smile was huge. It was time to write.

So, here's to coming along with me on my journey to self-love, self-discovery, and self-realization. Prepare yourself for the ride as I tell my story through emotions and feelings of **LOSS, LOVE, OBSTACLES,** and **VICTORY**. Ready or not, here we go!

LOSS

The Awareness Moment

Trauma Groomed

I grew up in an environment where my presence was too much.

My very existence was a burden, so I adjusted.

I became accommodating, bending, maneuvering, and easy to be around.

My personality demands attention, and my voice commands a presence.

So, you can imagine how difficult it was to shrink and muffle who I was and move about without a sound.

I taught myself as a child that to be worthy of love, I had to earn it.

I had to be a self-soother not to interrupt those meant to soothe.

I learned to hide in plain sight.

I heard every word, felt every emotion, and saw every fight.

I matured in an environment where I had contained myself, so much so that when it was ok to be me, I didn't know who that was.

Connected Conversations

So again, I adapted. This time I hid behind a tough exterior and managed to mimic those around me, and became whatever they needed me to be

Do you need a mother? I got you.

Do you need a sidekick? I got you.

Do you need someone to blame?

I got you there too.

I've played all these roles, and for the first time, I feel my most significant role is simply Tiffany.

I flourished in an environment where **trauma** consumed me, depression and anxiety groomed me, yet this is the environment I learned to speak up for myself and set boundaries for those chosen to be in my life.

In this stage, I learned that showing up for me is more important than shrinking to be more easily digestible for those who see me as "too much."

I created my (own) light and grew in an environment where growth seemed unattainable, and love seemed unreachable.

Trauma Groomed

Yet, I continued to grasp life's strings and turn those frail strings into a strong rope.

When I fall, I lift myself back up and look to God to find hope.

Second Chances

I wish second chances were (really) a thing.

I wish I could hear you laugh or laugh at you sing.

I wish we had more time to mend what had been broken for so long.

I miss what I never had and am tired of trying to convince myself I'm wrong.

There are so many things I never got to say because anger and life got in the way.

When you first passed, I felt hope exit my body.

I (quite literally) decided it didn't exist because I had hoped for so long to understand why you couldn't stay.

It was never made clear to me.

So, in my guilt and hatred, I felt protected. Thus, that's where I lay.

The night before, I flew to Atlanta to say goodbye.

I wrote you three different poems.

Connected Conversations

None were fitting to be shared in public spaces; too private of words, not meant for strangers' tear-soaked faces.

I wrote one for how much I hated you for not loving me.

I wrote the second for how much I longed to be the daughter you shared inside jokes.

I wished for more stories that showed me how a man is supposed to lead.

I wanted so badly to feel the warmth of femininity instead of the duty and burden of being resilient.

I wanted you to smile as you gave me away and say I know you picked the right one because you are brilliant.

I wrote the last for how sorry I was that I could not forgive you while you were still breathing.

I wrote about how much I hid behind my anger and that, in reality, I was just hurt.

Fighting for your attention was exhausting, disappointing, and, at best, embarrassing.

I wrote about how I used anger to protect my heart.

Second Chances

Then, amid writing, God sent you to comfort me as I described how your lack of love broke me.

I sat in the parking garage and felt embraced by your arms from the raindrops that started to fall.

The heavier the drops, the tighter your grip seemed.

I released myself from the guilt I had attached to my heart.

God spoke to me for the first time in a long time.

And now, a year later, I sit here remembering where and who I was that day.

I've grown so much since that time has passed.

I have found that we are all searching for something.

That something is usually at the tip of our tongue or the scope of our sight.

I lost you, but I reconnected with God that night.

Fooled

I thought I got lucky.

I met a man who had some consistency, and then boom, semi-ghosted with no real explanation, brought me back to reality.

We were vibing, and I was (really) starting to open up to you, but that was the problem.

I got too comfortable.

And apparently, feelings are wrong.

Or, (maybe) I should not talk about my feelings for you.

Act calm and unbothered so you don't run.

I thought I was special, but maybe it was all just fun.

I thought I got lucky.

I met a man with some consistency but then, wait, he caught feelings.

The moment he tells me is the exact moment he wants a break from me.

I mean, I know there are other factors at play.

Connected Conversations

I was (really) hopeful that you were not the norm and would communicate your hesitations, concur with them, and stay.

I thought I got lucky, but it's not as if I even believe in luck anyway.

Daddy Issues

Dear Dad,

I sit in the dark atop my bed with tear-smeared cheeks and sadden-soaked eyes while listening to the rain slide down the drain pipe.

I am thinking of you because, for some reason, I have dedicated my Sundays to thoughts of you and memories I have of love and family.

I even put in some memories that don't exist.

Sunday is my day.

It's the day I isolate myself to recharge for the week ahead.

Another week of smiling until I mean it and talking when I don't want to.

Sunday is my day to be.

It is my day to think or overanalyze without someone judging me for overthinking.

Sometimes it's my day to cry, and sometimes it's my day to laugh.

No matter which mood I am in, it's mine.

But today, it's not. It's yours.

Connected Conversations

I gave the day to you.

I watched movies with strong male leads that played imperfect fathers with perfect love for their daughters.

I watched movies with fathers that left with no explanation as to why and they never returned.

I tell everyone who asks me about you that I am over the past and forgave you.

I thought that if I said it enough, it would come true.

Seeing the power I gave you over my thoughts, feelings, and mood bothers me.

I am writing you to say that I don't hate you.

I (just) can't talk to you.

Quite frankly, I don't know you.

I am sorry that I can't be the daughter you want me to be, the one who pushes past the pain to endure the awkward silence so you can feel relieved from your guilt or comforted in your last months.

I want to be that person, but not for you, for me.

Because then that would be proof, right?

Daddy Issues

Proof that the past doesn't still have a hold of me.

When I hear your voice, it triggers memories of yelling and cruel words spoken to me while in your drunken stupor.

When I hear you speak, it triggers anger for the lies you have told yourself.

I can't believe you when you say you love me.

I can't bring myself to say those words to you.

Just because you are my father doesn't make those words true.

The struggle is that I can see what not having you around did to me.

I push people away before they start to go because I assume they will one day.

I yell when I should be tender because where I come from, tenderness gets you hurt and disappointed.

I pray to God that one day I will forgive you.

I wish that day could be today because I am tired of the melodramatic daddy issues.

Just Pull Back

Why is that so hard for me to do?

Why is it that when I think of you, I want to see, feel and hear you too?

Just pull back.

Why does that seem like an impossible task?

Why is me next to you all that, I ask?

I am afraid of being consumed by you, but I am sure I already am.

I dream of you and daydream about what kind of man you could be instead of living this reality where you tell me you are not him.

Just pull back.

You can't seem to provide me with the affection that I need.

So, please tell me.

Why am I here just letting my heart bleed?

You're Gonna Want Me Back

From the moment you were born, you played the waiting game. But you didn't know it.

It started with mom.

"I can't wait until she walks."

"I can't wait until she talks."

When asked about your age, you added "and a half" after the number as if that half meant you were smarter, faster, cooler, or more grown-up than your plain-old 4.

You longed to play with the big kids and have your bedtime extended.

You longed to talk and text unmonitored, so your little heart could be broken and mended.

"I can't wait until I can drive."

"I can't wait until I am grown."

"I can't wait to move away from home."

You said you couldn't wait.

So, I took away seconds, minutes, and hours every year.

You never even noticed.

Connected Conversations

Then, you hit your twenties.

Hours turned into days.

Then your thirties and days turned to months.

I gave you what you wanted, and now you want too much.

Slowing down after I have sped up is always harder, especially when I gave the brakes to you.

I sent you hints along the way.

Others who came before you said, "don't move too fast. It's gone in the blink of an eye."

Do you want to say you lived to die?

I can't slow down.

If I did, you would do it the same all over again.

Time is too precious to skip ahead and wish you caught the beginning, middle, and end.

I Woke Up Today

Today I awoke paralyzed by self-doubt and feelings of failure I cannot shake.

I lay in bed with salty tears slowly descending on my cheeks, wondering what would happen if I finally gave up on myself.

I woke up today.

That's a blessing, so I hear.

Yet living in this world is what I constantly and consistently fear.

Today I awoke paralyzed by self-hate and love for everyone who isn't me.

I awoke today upset at my (own) disappointment in opening my eyes.

I hate that I am so selfish.

Even though my leaving this earth would hurt the ones I love, I still awake some days wishing I hadn't.

My dark cloud hovers over me - all-knowing and condescending.

I thought I had gotten away but was reminded I did not today.

Connected Conversations

So, I run as the cloud gets darker and the water starts to fall.

Some days are better than others.

Sometimes I stop. I stare. I listen. I break my stride.

I feel the water flood my body, and I let it ride.

Some days I fall.

Dear Love

I am writing you again.

Hoping you feel my torture through this pen.

Despite the reflected grin, I am lost, you see.

You were everything I wanted.

Exactly what you are; I guess I don't truly know.

I fantasized about you from fabricated love stories and songs I thought to be true.

I loved you before I knew you, without knowing if I even believed in you.

I am writing you again.

Hoping you feel my torture through this pen despite the reflected grin.

I wonder about your existence from time to time.

I wonder if what I am yearning for is merely compiled words to a moving beat sung in a beautiful rhyme.

I wonder about you from time to time.

I hope that you feel my torture through this pen.

Connected Conversations

Look past my grin and into the depth of my eyes where secrets hide.

I hope that you will take pity on me and let me know you.

(Maybe) you will let me write my story and create my lyrics sung in beautiful rhymes.

I am lost, you see.

Show yourself to me and set this pain free.

Sincerely,

A beautiful grin with secrets of pain.

Take Note

Death taught me many lessons.

Like how the world keeps spinning and how important it is to appreciate your blessings.

It taught me to love and fight; I can't live life shifting between maybe and might.

Death taught me many lessons.

Many lessons about life

Like when you step outside and stop before rushing to the car, breathe. Close your eyes, and breathe.

Take note of how the balmy morning dew of Florida enriches your skin.

Take note of the people around you rushing. Smile. Say hello.

Appreciate the conversation that could happen and note the connections.

Death taught me many lessons.

And now I pay so much attention to how it is all connected.

October 26, 2022

I was not expecting my life to change with the passing of a man who was never involved in my life. Somehow my father's involvement in life had nothing to do with my grief, knowing we had run out of time. Now we will never be able to mend what was broken. Dad will never walk me down the aisle or meet my future kids. I was always aware of how important that was to me, but just how important I guess I had not (really) understood.

The trauma came from many places. Conversations with my therapist have taught me that just because I did not have it as bad as others does not mean it was not trauma. How can I love a man when I do not believe a man has ever loved me? I am starting to wonder if men are capable of the type of love I desire.

I realized, though, that this way of thinking is based merely on my belief that my father never loved me. So, if the only man supposed to love me unconditionally did not, how could any other man (love me) who has no ties to me? This same thinking is what I am trying to avoid. Or at least, so I thought.

In all reality, I would like to avoid time. We never have enough time. You know the saying, you can know someone for years and meet someone with better intentions. You spent years not being who you are. That was me. I spent six years of my life tied to someone I knew was incompatible with me. Why? Because it was safe and comfortable. Truthfully, I did not know what I wanted.

The only example had of love was from my sexy, sometimes raunchy love stories. I read about successful men wooing their women and making them feel special. I also blamed television and movies for my false sense of how a man loves a woman. Oh, and let us not forget R&B! I never saw what love looked like, but I was obsessed with what movies, songs, and books said it would feel like.

I was a feign for love. I wanted to be loved and be love all at the same time. Yet, I never learned how to love myself. Through losing my father and the size of a whole person, I started to love myself. I love the fat, loose skin, and all. I lost myself and found myself all at the same time. What are the lessons in loss? Love yourself, find yourself, and be yourself.

LOVE

In the Moment

Twin Flame

Thank you for allowing me to heal in the safety of your energy.

Thank you for helping me find myself.

I wasn't prepared for you and (truthfully) wasn't looking to find you.

I wasn't expecting to let myself get lost in you.

But here we are.

I did. It hurts when timing inevitably changes the trajectory of our soundtrack.

But what feels good is my faith in my bounce back.

Thank you for providing a safe space for me to open up truly.

Your peaceful presence and supportive demeanor helped me to be vulnerable.

And showed me how to put my needs first.

When things ended, I took the day to feel the loss of a new love and gained the confidence to continue loving the parts of me that aren't so appealing.

Connected Conversations

Where I thought the pain would stay, gratitude appeared, and to my surprise, the tears disappeared.

So, I want you to know that although things did not work out as we'd hoped, or maybe it was just me, I did gain something from our time together.

Confidence and more strength to endure heavy rains so that I remember to appreciate all the gains.

Five Steps To Loving Me

Love yourself first. Do your (own) inner work.

Please get to know the real me so you can see my worth.

Because at some point, I will need a reminder.

There are times when I am blind to my beauty.

Be honest in your intent.

Be truthful to your feelings and communicate your consent of discontent.

Know that I will need reassurance and extra attention on my anxious days.

Listen to my voice and read my face.

Be patient to understand the things I don't say.

Trust yourself enough to let me in.

When you're ready and feel like I can handle your burdens, no matter how heavy, laugh with me.

Not every day will be sunny, and not everything will be funny.

But be the reason I find the strength to curl my lips up and laugh until I cry.

Connected Conversations

Be open enough to allow me in so that I can reciprocate.

As they say, laughter is the best medicine.

I'll repeat step 1 to make sure it sinks in.

Love yourself first. Do your (own) inner work.

Know that, at times, I will need to lean on you to show me my worth.

You may be blind to the beauty within you.

I will keep a mirror on me to show you the reflection I see.

<u>Lucky One</u>

I thought I got lucky.

I met a man with some consistency, and then boom. I was semi-ghosted with no real explanation.

His disappearance brought me right back to reality.

We were vibing. I was starting to open up to you, but that was the problem.

I got too comfortable.

And apparently, feelings are wrong, or don't talk about my feelings for you act cool and unbothered, so you don't run.

I thought I was special, but maybe it was all just fun.

I thought I got lucky.

I met a man with some consistency, but then wait. He caught feelings. The moment he tells me is the exact moment he wants a break from me.

I mean, I know there are other factors at play.

I hoped you were different from the norm and could communicate your hesitations, concur with them, and stay.

Connected Conversations

I thought I got lucky.

But it is not as if I even believe in luck anyway.

November 22, 2022

Dating sucks! Is love real? What the fuck am I doing?

I have been on a slew of dates, and by slew, I mean maybe one a week with different guys. I FINALLY had a third date with the same guy. He is nice enough, but I don't know if I like him. I mean, he checks the boxes. Well, he checks the boxes my friends tell me he should check, which may not necessarily be my boxes.

He is shorter than me with my heels on. Besides what could be deemed superficial, he has shared how limited his time is. I realized that time was a big deal for me. I spent most of my life chasing time and trying to steal bits and pieces from my dad, who never had enough time for me. Now that I am older, I realize how little time we have on this earth, not to mention that my biological clock is ticking so loud in my head. So how could I not obsess over time or lack thereof?

I was in Cali three weeks ago, and my time with my siblings helped me remember what love was. So I know it is real. I don't know at this moment the level of attainability it holds for me with somebody's son out here in this world.

Connected Conversations

Through conversation with my brother Eric and his wife Allison, we discussed the importance of being picky about whom you choose to spend your time, space, and energy. Eric told me how proud he was of my level of growth from vulnerability. Mind you, this is my little brother, but he is wise beyond his years. He told me it has been difficult to find someone I like because I finally started loving the right person. That person is me. I spent so much time trying to make sure someone else liked me that I didn't know myself, so how could I like myself? Now that I have opened up space for myself and gotten to know who I am, I have realized how much I love who I am, how I am, what I do, and how I do it. I am so comfortable with myself that I refuse to be uncomfortable in anyone's space.

I like myself, and (for me) to like somebody's son, they will have to make me like me even more than I already do to love them the way I want and the way I want to be loved.

Choices

I'm not even gonna lie.

I be wanting to be in love.

From the first conversation, I want my heart to skip a beat and my stomach to have butterflies.

Why?

Well, I was taught to believe love is an innate feeling when (really) it's a choice.

Love is saying yes to someone you may have usually said no to.

Love is slowly getting to know someone's personality based on what they show you.

Love is choosing to be curious enough to want to know more.

Love is choosing what areas of their personality resonate with yours.

I'm not even gonna lie.

I be wanting to be in love @ hello.

And when I am, choosing not to run.

I want to know about past traumas and their insecurities. Thus, I can avoid wasting time

Connected Conversations

dealing with someone who doesn't know, isn't working on it, or doesn't care.

In doing so, I won't repeat the mistake of realizing this person isn't willing to work on themselves after I have caught feelings for them and seen their red flags.

I thought I was done healing, but I forgot one trauma.

I forgot the trap and allure of instant connection.

I expect every interaction to resemble that connection; if it doesn't, I'm out.

But I have learned that just as fast as it started is how quickly it will burn.

So, if I want it to last, I must **choose** patience, **choose** grace, and **choose** the love that fits what I deserve.

Love is not this magically instant connection.

That's deception and lessons wrapped up in a bow.

Love is a conscious choice to be made daily.

Choices

We must first **choose** to let our guard down and start with a blank sheet of expectations and fill them in as we go.

Luminescent Light

Sometimes you (just) gotta look up at the sky and stare.

And when you do, hopefully, you are greeted by the luminescent ring surrounding the moon, inviting you in.

Allowing you to dream;

Allowing you to wander;

Allowing you to lust;

Sometimes when the moon beckons your imagination and commands you to explore, you oblige.

As I sit here in this public place with the cool, moist breeze comforting and calming the fire that builds inside me, I can't help but envision your eyes staring down into mine.

Low, caring, open, and wanting.

Somehow, gusts of wind enveloping me feel like your breath on my neck.

The faint sound of the crowd bustling below me sounds like the whisper of my name from your lips.

I close my eyes to savor the vision for as long as the moon's light allows.

Connected Conversations

Sometimes you (just) gotta look up at the sky and let the moon remind you, entice you, and then you will let go.

November 25, 2022

Does dating suck, or am I just doing it wrong? I pose this question when, honestly, I know the answer. Yes, dating does suck. I know this from experiences and conversations with other men and women who would agree. However, just because dating sucks does not mean love does.

I met someone today at work who was fine. When I say fine, I mean drop-dead gorgeous. Tall. Ya'll know how important that quality is to me. Pretty teeth. A sparkling smile, and of course, a wedding ring. His personality was like mine. Very outgoing, and no conversation was off limits.

For whatever reason, we established a friendship connection immediately. He was just one of those types of people like myself. He told me about his new wife and how he was about to book her the honeymoon of her dreams. His enthusiasm so enthralled me. He then asked me about my love life, to which I replied, "what love life?" He looked at me in shock, saying, "surely you have someone?" You are gorgeous, smart, and successful.

Following his compliment, he stated that he and his wife met on bumble when she was 36 and he 42. So, he quickly took back his comment and related with me on how hard it is to find someone to like, let alone love, in this age of social media and online speed dating. He told me how they matched on accident. Her dog swiped on her, and she told him it wasn't her. I laughed out loud at that. Gotta love it. Sis kept it real. But maybe, her dog was on to something because that was the last swipe she made.

He told me they both were swiping out of boredom at this point, but they were still open to a possibility. While I believe dating does suck and finding love is difficult, one must keep cultivating and believing in the possibility of LOVE. Doing so is key.

This lovely specimen of a man and I said our goodbyes, and I remember feeling a glimmer of hope in my stomach. I am certain he had no idea what that conversation did for me, but it is just another reminder of how it is all connected.

I don't think we are supposed to find LOVE. I believe LOVE finds us. Each time love found me, I grew. My mindset changed. My thoughts are processed at a more intricate level taking into account more perspectives than just my own, and if only for that, I am grateful to the men who came and left. Thank you for leaving me better than where you found me.

December 12, 2022

I'm sitting at one of my favorite spots wishing you were with me. I want to feel your love's warmth as the breeze rushes over me. I am longing for you, mad at you, and wondering why it's so damn hard to find you. I sit here looking out at the water that resembles glass and the scenery that promotes peace in an otherwise chaotic world, with the cars zooming by on the opposite side of the highway.

I breathe deeply to hold back the tears forming in my eyes. My gaze hardens, and I wipe them away quickly as I don't want a reminder of how pitiful I am. I am hell-bent on wanting to be loved by you, and I have no clue who you are or if you are real. It's as crystal clear as this water beneath my feet, but the love I want is not meant for me. When will I realize that you don't exist? You are merely a collection of love songs, fabricated stories, and sappy movies I have on repeat. You don't exist in that capacity, and I look for you in all the wrong people for whatever reason. So, I gave up. If I can't find you in the real world, I'll settle for you only in the confines of my imagination.

I've grown to love myself enough that if I don't find you, I will be all right. I can settle for being happy and content with a broken heart. I say this to say that it's all bullshit. I can't live without love. My being IS love. I was put on this earth to love and be loved.

I was having a conversation today with a very handsome stranger whom I hope won't continue to be a stranger, but with how I seem to attract temporary people, one never knows. This stranger and I talked for three hours, and the one thing that stuck with me was that if you are still trying to find love, that means you still believe in love, and if you still believe in love, that means you're not broken. You've been bent out of shape but can always snap back into shape. I'm sure he has no idea the levity those words held for me.

As I sat in this beautiful place feeling pitiful yet still believing love was out there for me, it dawned on me that (in reality) this shows my strength, resilience, and ability to be bent but never broken. I refuse to live with a broken heart because I chose faith. My heart was not meant to be alone or loved in half measure. I will continue to love the temporary people and appreciate the lessons they teach me and the love they show me until I am ready for my permanent person. They are waiting to ensure I know my strength and trust that I will not be broken.

OBSTACLES

The Boundaries Moment

Hi Mom

Hi Mom, I squeak, barely above a whisper.

Over the railing, looking down at this beautiful mess, I call mom.

She doesn't hear me.

Her balance is challenged by her green pet plant, placed beautifully to the left of our front door.

Down she goes.

I started to run down the stairs to help her, but I stopped as I heard sniffles that did not sound like physical pain.

The sniffles sounded like she was broken.

They sounded like this mess on the floor of our rented foyer. She was defeated.

They sounded like her tear drops which were going to make puddles on the floor.

Puddles which I would have to clean.

They sounded like fear.

Connected Conversations

When she finally noticed me staring at her in pain, she wiped her eyes and smiled.

Mom said, "Hi Baby."

That night, I learned that smiles look like doubt.

Breathe

Suck it in, arch your back, and smile wide, so they don't notice the fat.

Hair out, chin up, and hand on your hip covering the marks.

That's right, just like that.

I hide behind my gorgeous smile that tells a lie, saying I am confident and sure of myself.

I suck it in to take a picture or to walk down the street to ensure I do not hear the whispers such as, "Omg, look at her."

One of these days, I'll breathe.

I'll loosen up a little. Inhale and breathe.

I'll let my breath back out when I find myself.

I'll make a change.

The time for change is not tomorrow; it's today.

So, today I'll breathe.

Connected Conversations

I'll let it hang.

Because tomorrow I'll make sure it's gone.

Why? So that I never have to suck it in again.

Today I'll breathe.

I'll smile at the truth, knowing I am more than just my pretty face.

I'll breathe. I'll sweat. I will hurt to be healthy and add confidence to my never-ending list of attributes.

The time for change is today.

Why? To stop the whispers I hear from others, but most importantly, to stop the whispers in my mind telling me I am not enough.

Today I'll breathe.

Breathe

The day I was kicked off of a ride at an amusement park.

Weight: 375 lbs

Connected Conversations

Photoshoot nine months after the day at the amusement park.

Weight: 275

Breathe

Photoshoot nine months after the day at the amusement park.

Weight: 275

Roller Coaster

I can't shut off my brain.

My emotions got a hold of my thoughts, and everything I thought I knew somehow got tossed out the window far away from my brain.

When the teeth of my emotions sink in, I throw away such things as logic.

It feels like chaos and euphoria all at the same time.

I can't get off this roller coaster of mine.

I'm falling longer, faster, deeper, but yeah, you know it's all fine.

I can't shut off my mind.

Emotions took the reins.

I am a prisoner in my (own) brain.

December 29, 2022

(I am) sitting atop my queen size bed that I wish was a king because then it could fit all of me. When I say all of me, I mean all my racing thoughts, my heart rate that goes up 100 beats per min too many times to count, and my tears that I can't stop from falling. I am wondering (again) if my existence is too much. If who I am, what I do, and how I act are too much. I have been told on several occasions that my attitude or my enthusiasm is too much. Or my mother's favorite, "Tiffany, you are so dramatic." Being told that you are too much by one too many people of importance in your life has a way of making you believe that you are. For a person with bipolar disorder, being too much makes you feel like you don't belong. It makes you feel as though you're a burden to the important people around you.

The first time I wrote a suicide note was to my mother at the age of 11. I kept it in a purple velvet journal. It held my secrets and my pain. My mom never saw the letter, but I saved it for a down day. I kept my tears to myself, and they were easily brushed off as "Tiffany's just sensitive." It was (and still is) a running joke in my family. Little did anyone know that I have a chemical imbalance in my brain where I feel things more extreme than I should.

Connected Conversations

I was first diagnosed with bipolar disorder at the age of 28 after a bad breakup with my on-again-off-again love. I wanted answers for my overt display of emotions. The answers I got led me to uncover that I had a mood disorder. While I felt relieved to have an answer, when sharing it with my friends and family, some seemed apprehensive about believing it. It seemed they just thought it was an excuse to excuse my behavior. So, I constantly went off my meds, believing I was not bipolar. I visited different psychiatrists, and they tested me repeatedly with the same result. I have finally concluded that I am (bipolar), and I have to find a way to cope as we all do.

Life is coping. For me, coping looks a lot like this - writing. Writing saved me, and reading other people's emotions in the art form of writing where I could have someone relate to me was also life-changing. It was important for me to be a part of that. Another aspect of coping for me was eating. Eating became a way to be social, allowing me to find solace in the fullness of a meal. I was told at a young age to eat all my food or else, even if I was eating past the point of feeling full. This belief measure has stayed with me. I have been bigger (than most) since age 11.

The Boundaries Moment

I never felt comfortable in my (own) skin, and I never felt like my skin belonged to me. So at the age of 30, I finally decided to make a change. I put myself first and was going to prove it this time. After being asked to get off a ride at Disney's Animal Kingdom, I cried in humiliation as my niece and her mom witnessed the embarrassing ordeal. I called my boyfriend at the time crying, and his attitude screamed, "well, duh, why'd you even try to get on?" Or at least that was what my mind was telling me. That was the last day I would spend not feeling 100% like myself.

I decided to make an appointment with my doctor, and we discussed the options of weight loss surgery, and I started the process of my weight loss journey. I lost a whole overweight person and found me. I became open-minded, willing to listen, and learned the perspective of others while still maintaining my individuality. In my weight, I hid behind the opinions of others as if they were my thoughts. When I shed that weight, I was introduced to a Tiffany that I began to like. I discovered a Tiffany that took risks, hiked, went white water rafting, joined camp gladiator, and pushed herself. I began to become someone I liked.

Non-Responsive

When asked, "what's wrong," and I don't respond, it's because I don't fucking know.

I don't know why the comment infuriated me and why certain looks caused my body to shudder.

I don't know what's wrong.

I don't know if it's because of what or how it was said.

I just know I have run to get away from it.

So, unresponsive I become.

I hide out in my bedroom and ignore the world for however long I can until I have to reemerge in the real world, force a smile, and through gritted teeth, whisper, "I'm fine."

Emptiness followed me everywhere I ran.

I am trapped in this bubble of temporary highs, temporary people, and permanent lows.

I sometimes wish to stay trapped, so I never have to fake a smile again.

Connected Conversations

Other times I wish I wasn't so damn needy, opening my heart to anyone who claims they need me.

This bubble doesn't protect me.

It hurts me.

This bubble traps me, and it never lets me go.

So when you ask me what's wrong, believe me when I say I don't fucking know.

<u>Goodbye</u>

Usually, on this day, I lay in bed and fight back tears all day.

Then around midnight, I stop fighting and let them fall.

I can't tell you exactly why.

Words can't describe it at all.

It's been about two weeks without the unbeknownst sadness that hovers ominously over me.

My personal dark cloud, isn't she so lovely?

The last two weeks were great.

I was inspired and filled with life.

Yet, today I feel nothing but strife.

That's the stupid game of this bipolar life.

The chemical in my brain tricked me into thinking I was some semblance of happy.

Then they capture me, leaving me stuck.

Connected Conversations

To go through life with my eyes wide open when all I want is to live life manic with my eyes shut.

Or live my life without giving so many fucks.

I want to say goodbye to every emotion throughout the day.

Leave them in a box on an airport runway.

I'd rather feel nothing.

After all, numbness never hurt anyone anyway.

Goodbye to these feelings that covet me.

Hello to nothing.

In you, I hope to feel free.

January 5, 2023

I am in beautiful Hawaii on the eve of my birthday. I am sitting on my mother's 14th-floor balcony, looking out at the Ala Wai Canal with picturesque mountain views to my left and beautiful city and ocean views to my right. I am reminded of how far I have come and thinking of the people who helped me get here.

A conversation comes to mind that I had with my baby sister when she was living 30 minutes away from me. Boy, I sure do miss that. I divulged to my family that I was diagnosed as bipolar. Unbeknownst to me, Erika researched to understand more about the disorder. Honestly, I am quite positive she understands it better than me. She picked topics in school around mood disorders to see how she could better understand me. She told me this on a Sunday fun day that was ruined by the dark cloud of anxiety brewing over my head. I cried and apologized profusely for being the "mood killer." She just hugged me. This was a pivotal moment because my sister is not a hugger. Erika told me that there was no reason for me to apologize to her for feeling what I felt. She helped me understand that I couldn't help it but could fight it by being honest about who I am. I cried it out and immediately felt a release.

Connected Conversations

We discussed other things, reminisced, and spent time in nature on the Tampa Bay Riverwalk. Why was this moment so pivotal? I often refer to this moment in my alone time as the time I truly accepted my diagnosis, spoke about it openly, and was honest with the fact that the chemicals in my brain shift my moods, and it's not my fault.

However, what I could control, I wasn't. I was not taking my medication as prescribed. I expected to return to normal as if normal was a possibility. This was the first time I realized how my lack of care for my (own) mental well-being affected those around me who loved me. I wish I could say I never went off my meds again after this moment, but I can not. I went off several times and truthfully, even as this journal entry is being written.

I have been on them for 10 consecutive days. This is a record for me over the last year. I struggle with taking them because my creative side is halted, making me feel apart from normal people. Like why do I have to take medication just to be balanced?

Truthfully, I have not felt balanced since birth. I am not sure that the medicine even works, but (to be fair) I have not been consistent enough to truly give it a shot. I want to feel what

The Boundaries Moment

it would be like not to have thoughts racing every second and to not second guess every decision, question every tone, or switch my body language from those around me.

The conversation I had with my sister that day reminded me that what I can control is how I face my obstacles. I can let the obstacles happen or control how I react to them. I can use tools, resources, and the community to support me. I can speak up. I can cry to let it out so I can breathe. I CAN BE HONEST. In all of that comes freedom.

VICTORY

The Decisive Moment

Rescue Rope

Thinking of you brings a smile to my lips that I don't recognize.

One that starts on my mouth, but it brings happiness that fills my eyes.

One of those smiles you feel from the inside.

I hadn't realized how long it's been since I felt a smile like that.

Not until you hugged me.

The last thing on my mind was letting go.

Or when you looked at me as if you (quite literally) could see through the walls I created to protect me from loving you.

Thinking of you brings a calmness to the storm that brews never ending in my head.

Knowing that I am free to feel whatever I want, I can express myself to you instead.

Thinking of you brings a smile to my lips that I hadn't realized was a possibility.

Your desire to see me whole provided me visibility.

Connected Conversations

Your patience showed me strength, and your kindness gave me hope.

Your faith became my rope as I grasped for air while drowning.

I don't know how I could ever repay you for the solace your love provides, but thank you for showing me through love how God guides me.

In my heart is where yours resides.

Always Turn The Page

I love hard, unfortunately.

Even when the only thing it does is hurt me.

Once you finally get my full attention, I am sold.

I have already pictured our lives together, growing old, you know, gray-haired and slow-moving.

The whole nine.

Because when I look into your eyes after all those years, I still know you are mine.

I can't wait for that breathtaking, forever kinda love.

To know I will always be wanted with just one hug.

To know I will always be protected with just one kiss.

To know I will always be safe with just one look.

I love hard, unfortunately.

Connected Conversations

The only thing it does is hurt me, but I refuse to let my broken heart disable me.

I know real love is out there.

Even if I haven't experienced love, when that someone loves you back.

I take the blame for not feeling that.

I never took the time to love myself.

Otherwise, I would have already experienced love.

The thought of love envelopes and (now) encourages me.

I will always turn the next page because now I know love knows me.

Always Turn The Page

Left side: Weight 375 | Right Side: Weight 183

Connected Conversations

Left side: Weight 275 | Right Side: Weight 183

Always Turn The Page

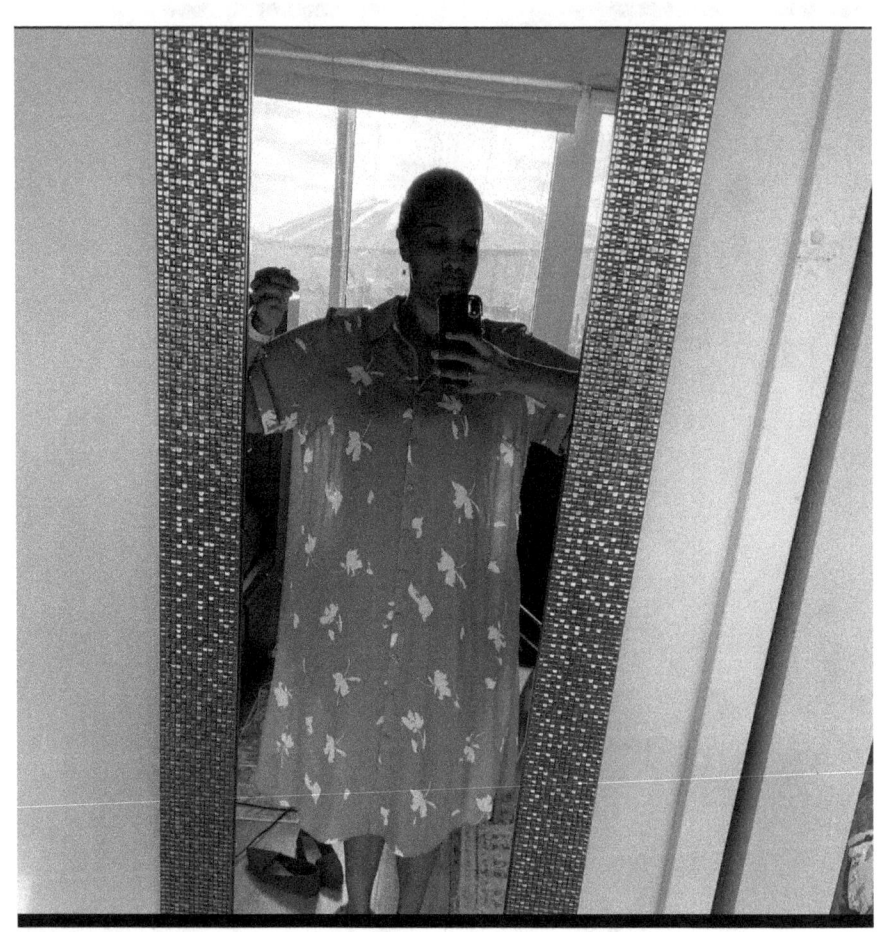

I LOST A WHOLE PERSON!

January 22, 2023

"Hello. Yes. I'm here." I say quickly while struggling to take the phone off mute and wipe away the remnants of strawberries and a protein shake that abruptly left my body. It was July 2019, two months after gastric sleeve surgery, and I was down 63 lbs. I am reminded of this memory in particular because when speaking to my older sister, Amber, I described how I felt when an employee, who happened to be in the room with me as I choked up my breakfast, decided to express her concern. She said, "all this just to be beautiful." At that moment, I said nothing while feeling ashamed from her perception of my vanity. I just stared and proceeded with the conference call, wishing my upchuck had landed on her out-of-date shoes.

While conversing with my sister, we discussed the 30 lbs I put back on and my plan to lose them again. She quickly reminded me that loving my body isn't conditional on how many pounds I have lost. To succeed on this journey I embarked on in 2019, I had to love my body first. To change, I had to first appreciate where I was and what my body did for me. I wish I had said that to my employee. I could have said, "no, all this was not to be beautiful." First, because I already was and still am beautiful.

Second, it was to prove to myself that I loved my body enough to do what it takes to make sure it's healthy, can sustain a lifestyle for me that keeps me active, and helps me hold my head up high as I do things I once thought were limitations with the weight I was lugging around.

Now, I hike, go for long walks, and don't notice how long until I see the sun setting. I went white-water rafting and mountain wall climbing. Finally, I could get on a plane without feeling the anxiety of asking for a seatbelt extender. I wish I knew how to voice to her all I allowed my body to endure for these changes to reap the benefit of using it to live my life.

What matters is that I know my choice was right for me, and I see what it did for my life. I have no regrets. Amber reminded me that I was not loving my body as I did when the weight first came off. In this conversation, my mindset expanded to the understanding that if I love my body like I say I do, then why do I not take my vitamins and work my muscles as I should? It isn't about losing the weight I gained back, but about taking care of my body and showing that I appreciate it through gains. The overall purpose is to use the correct dietary alignment, work out to feel better and be stronger, not lose weight, and fit into the jeans. Unfortunately, I had lost sight of this.

So, cheers sissy, for helping me grow. Here's to loving the 30 lbs I've put on since losing 183 lbs. Here's to focusing on loving where I am and working toward transforming my body into a strong temple of resilience. Finally, here's to relying on my body to take me on new adventures I never considered possible.

Vulnerability

Vulnerability is strength, or so I keep hearing.

I can't tell when it's vulnerability or the trauma response of oversharing.

I thought I was an open book. I divulge all of myself when getting to know people. I open up and let them in.

They sink. I fall. They don't know how to swim.

When is it vulnerability vs. oversharing?

Is it when I show all my cards too soon?

Some call that premature. I call it daring.

It doesn't take long to see who is right or wrong.

Mostly because I only like the wrong ones, as you can see.

Vulnerability is strength, or so I keep hearing.

Who draws the line as I cross over into oversharing?

I share all of me. No walls. No pretenses.

If you want to know something, just ask.
I give all of me.

Connected Conversations

But really, I speak on everything to see who can stick it out.

If I am going to be "too much" later, I might as well be it now.

If I am being honest, it's not me being vulnerable. It's that I don't believe I genuinely know how.

I share so much in hopes they'll run.

In the running, they don't (truly) see me having to be everything I say I am.

I am emotional and, at times, insecure, hard-headed, and outspoken.

I care to a fault, some say.

If I don't give them a chance to (truly) see this side of me, I save myself from actual rejection.

February 4, 2023

I have realized that I was not as open to love as I once was. As I sit here looking out the window of my 7th-floor apartment, I'm struggling with the thought that maybe I'm the toxic one. On the other hand, maybe my openness so soon was a way to protect myself from real rejection. I realized that either I was picking the same guy over and over again, or I'm saying no to the guy to whom I should probably say yes. If it's not one of those two options, there's a third. I'm sharing way too much information too soon. Let me set the stage.

It's a breezy night. To me, breezy means freezing. It's an unfortunate side effect I got after losing a whole person. I am cold ALL the time! Anyway, I met up with a stranger who was completely opposite of whom I usually date. I thought that this would help me get out of my way. My typical guy, as you know, is tall. Being tall is (obviously) a necessity for my 5'9" stature, but also dark and handsome. I typically like dimples too. Well, this guy was tall, with blue eyes, and (kind of) cute in an "I want to hug you and pinch your cheeks kind of way."

Connected Conversations

Through our conversation, we start to discuss topics like mental health. One of my favorite topics, but typically one I can get heated about quickly. He was sharing with me how he thinks his mother has been depressed his whole life and how his childhood trauma reflects in him as he navigates adulthood and relationships. I could tell from how he communicated that he was still actively dealing with his trauma, which affected his confidence and ability to maintain a career. He is so busy trying to prove to his parents that he is not the stupid kid they proclaimed him to be. However, in doing so, he is limiting himself and not seeing his potential beyond discussing dreams with a call to action.

My assessment could be wrong, but remember, this is a first impression. First impressions are everlasting, but entirely possible to change if I give him a second chance on another date, which I had already decided I would not do. The topic of depression struck a nerve within me, and I decided to share that I was bipolar. This was not the first time I have shared being bipolar on a first date. The moment I share that, I know I have checked out. That overshare is a way for me to either not have to deal with rejection when they find out later and decide that I am "too emotional." Or, it's an out for me if I decide they are "too nice." In this case, I felt this stranger didn't have the emotional capacity to deal with someone like me. I could have been wrong, and honestly, I probably was. But we will never know.

In analyzing this date, like I do most of them, I have decided that, at times, I am the toxic counterpart, and I am the problem. I didn't give him a chance, and I made decisions about him based on my past experiences with exes or traumas. Unfortunately, these past experiences seem to keep rearing their ugly heads in the form of imposter syndrome. They have held me back from promotions and positions for which I was qualified or maybe even overqualified.

So, my toxic trait is that I prejudge people based on those who have hurt me in the past, and sometimes that's even myself. However, I am a fully self-aware individual, at least today at this very moment. Victory lies in my ability to see past the toxic traits of others. Victories won are not always in something easy to see, like losing

180 lbs. or finally leaving the job you hated and landing one you love. But, sometimes, the victory is as big as seeing your (own) faults, working toward acknowledging them and being the change you wish you saw in others.

So, in the spirit of change and growth, I texted him to say we wouldn't work instead of just ghosting. Don't judge. That was a huge win for the past Tiffany. While being self-aware, I recognize where I could be the problem but also that I would know if someone were for me.

In my wins, my mindset has grown. I have greater self-awareness, and I am unafraid to call myself out. I have also learned to trust my instincts, which is huge because, in overthinking and second-guessing myself, you would think I believed my subconscious had bad intentions for me.

Today, however, I will bask in the challenge won and learned from my revelations. Lessons learned:

1. Oversharing is a trauma response and does not mean open.

2. Trust yourself. You know what you want.

The Decisive Moment

3. Being self-aware and accountable for your thought is your biggest win!

January 16, 2023

Crack goes the crab legs as I break into them to capture and savor the meat within. The way that came out sounded kind of dirty. Well, that is not where I am going. I am drying up tears and trying to get my act together.

It's 80 degrees. The wind is blowing. The sound of the waves caresses the air, and I am here crying over my hair. Or at least that's what I claim when speaking to my beautiful silver-haired mother across the table. Alas, Tanya (my mother) calls bullshit. She knows all, and you cannot get much past her, especially when it is one of her flock. She gets me more now than she ever has. Her understanding of me makes me feel seen, more visible than ever before. We have grown so much in our relationship that I can openly express that I can't pinpoint exactly what's wrong, just that every muscle in my body is tight and clenched, waiting for the other shoe to drop—waiting for life, as I know it, to end. Exactly why I feel that way, I can't say because I don't know where these thoughts come from. But she hears me, feels, and sees me in her clarity.

I released the tears that had been building up but trapped for days since I arrived in Hawaii. The growth in our relationship from one year to the next is incredible. That goes to show the individual work we both did. I remember feeling like this two years ago when she visited me in Florida. I couldn't openly communicate my emotions, and this frustrated her so much that all she wanted to do was get away from the negative energy that was permeating off of me. My car had gotten a flat, which doesn't seem like a big deal, but I had been dealing with car issues draining my pockets for months. So instead of talking it through with me or trying to understand what seemed an irrational response, she ran as fast as possible in the other direction of my 450 square-foot studio we had been sharing while she visited.

She is in life's transition with her move to New Jersey from California. I am sure it all felt like a step backward and forward all at the same time. This moment brought me back to feelings of unimportance or how I was "too much to be around." So, this is the story I told myself. Once again, I was too much to want to be around, see, or even understand.

Back to the present time in Hawaii, my mother expressed how it's ok not to be able to explain what's causing the tears. It's ok to just "be." If you need to cry, then cry. There's no pressure to explain why. This is such a far cry from two years ago, and I realized therein lies the victory.

Connected Conversations

The victory is always growth in oneself that allows growth in whatever relationship you deem important. We discussed being in the moment and knowing how hard this is for me. I attempted to have this peace for the rest of my time in Hawaii. Yet, I found myself ruining my trip by living outside the moment, whether in the past or the future.

Beyond the hard shell we use to protect ourselves, if we put in the work, we inevitably get to the tender meat we intend to savor. I smiled while moving from my crab legs to my favorite dessert, Crème Brulee. I savored the sweetness and knew I would forever hold this moment in my heart.

So, in the spirit of living in the present, I decided - at this moment - I would enjoy these three c's - Compassion, Crab legs, and Crème Bruleé.

About the Author

Tiffany Street grew up knowing and recognizing, by age 9, life was a river constantly moving, always ebbing and flowing. After sharing her very first poem with her Pop Pop, who, after hearing it, was deeply impressed by her level of thought and how his 9-year-old granddaughter was able to convey her thoughts, he encouraged her never to stop writing. Tiffany writes what makes her laugh, cry, cringe, and love without limits but with plenty of hesitation. However, she is reminded of what her Pop Pop shared that day. So, in doing the right thing, she listened to her elders, leading to her first book. As seen in *Connected Conversations*, if you feel it write it.

www.ingramcontent.com/pod-product-compliance
Lightning Source LLC
Chambersburg PA
CBHW060351170426
43202CB00029B/2864